STREET CAKE

experimental writing prize

winners' anthology

2021

EDITED BY

NIKKI DUDLEY

&

TRINI DECOMBE

Published in the United Kingdom in 2021
by streetcake magazine
124 Cadogan Terrace, London, E9 5HP.

First printing, 2021

ISBN 978-1-8380-9602-1

Cover design by Trini Decombe
Typesetting by Alec Newman Book Design
alecnewman.kfs@gmail.com

contents

contents

We are extremely happy to have been able to deliver our experimental writing prize for the third time in 2021, building on the successes of the previous years and also learning a lot in order to move forward and grow. We are so pleased ACE saw fit to fund our prize and celebrate innovative writing and those producing it, especially in such competitive times.

We're seeing more and more love for experimental writing, and lots of new journals and presses popping up, which makes us extremely happy! We want more people to see how amazing innovative writing is. The only issue we have now is that we have so much amazing work to choose from that it can be a very challenging process running a prize! We want everyone to know that we appreciate you trusting us with your work and we are so pleased you wanted to be involved with our prize.

The prize has seen some development this year. We are delivering more mentoring to the second and third placed winners, which will be delivered by ourselves. We hope this will expand the opportunities for development to more writers and give them more sustained support. Moreover, we also opened up the prize to everyone over 18 and those who are resident in the UK and EU, which was a massive step, but one which we hoped would open up the prize to more people at different stages of their writing career, and also expand our international links. Both have proved to be true.

The last big change was the removal of the £1 entry fee. Instead we held a raffle, where lots of our generous partners offered amazing prizes for a £3 entry. We had a lot of happy winners and were also able to cover most of the fee removal. Moreover, we introduced a voluntary donation button and we want to thank those who felt able to use this and support our prize, especially for the benefit of those who may have struggled to pay to enter. The sense of community has been absolutely amazing and we can't thank you enough!

We would also like to acknowledge the support of all the organisations who shared news of the prize and supported our work. Furthermore, we want to thank ACE for funding this project and the writers we reach. Our judges have all been incredibly helpful and supportive as ever: Anita Goveas, Karenjit Sandhu, Jarred McGinnis and Astra Papachristodoulou. Big thanks also to: Isabelle Kenyon and Fly on the Wall Press, Haley

Jenkins and Selcouth Station Press, SJ Fowler, Writers' Centre Kingston, Leone Ross, Joe Ruddock, Simon Cusack, Sascha Akhtar, Alec Newman of KFS Press, Untitled Writing, Sam Ruddock, and everyone else who has supported our work and sent us good vibes throughout.

We can't wait for you to enjoy the range of innovative and emotive work we have for you this year. We're really proud of all the writers included and we hope you'll be seeing a lot more of them and their writing!

We hope you enjoy the writing in this anthology as much as we do. Thank you for reading.

Nikki and Trini

Managing Editors, streetcake

seams of juvenilia

I don't know where to begin /
day after day / ascension is deep
down in the soil / seams of stones /
womb / encased in violets /
waiting / to climb out of the lake /
dripping replica / scavenged /
torture / walls / ripped machine /
memories / caving / shapeless
power / this place / burrowed pain
not ours / I can't / uncover /
swept toads / they say /
serenity drifts / on the other side /
but / I see / no boat /

hemmed
in
hemmed
in
hemmed
in
hemmed
in
hemmed
in
hemmed
in
hemmed
in
hemmed
in
hemmed
in
hemmed
in
hemmed
in
hemmed
in
hemmed
in
hemmed
in
hemmed
in
hemmed
in
hemmed
in
hemmed
in
hemmed
in
hemmed
in
hemmed
in
hemmed
in
hemmed
in
hemmed
in
hemmed
in
hemmed
in
hemmed
in
hemmed
in
hemmed
in
hemmed
in
hemmed
in
hemmed
in
hemmed
in
hemmed
in
hemmed
in
hemmed
in
hemmed
in
hemmed
in
hemmed
in

ghost wood

The New Year's Eve after my dad died, I went into the woods behind his old house to walk the join between the years. Before the birds were awake, before branches and the last few leaves bent in a crown of noise, I stood in a blue room of trees. Out of a crease in the moor where hill meets hill came mist out of the plain air – something up ahead: a rustle, bootsteps dampened by mud, a head on a human spine twisting itself alive. And the fear I felt was so strong it was almost genital, almost desire. Real trees around an unreal man. A real man still walking this unreal valley over the ridge where the branches bend and hush, come back to stillness. No bootsteps, no blue wood: all memory

POETRY
30 AND UNDER

云吞

lit. cloud swallow — a migration of birds blading the horizon

Deluxe Green Bo   New York City, NY
$5.90 for 5

Poons'   London, UK
£10 for 5

Danwei Canting   Portland, OR
$9 for 7

Fortune Garden   Vancouver, BC
$8.50 for a small

Three Fold Noodles   Little Rock, AK
$9.89 for a regular

Hot Wok   Lyon, FR
€3.80 for 3

NAME

DEPART   **FLIGHT**

ARRIVE   **GATE**

DATE   **TIME**   **SEAT**

Name a past
                    ready
      to depart
                          a flight   and   a life.
            An arrival hall
without   room
      for living.
                          At the boarding gate,
                                                date
every   season.   Fold your

                timezones
      under the
            seat.

Name, a past
tense, like family waving
in the rearview mirror while
you clutch a cold sandwich
from Pret, the supersized chain for
ready-made meals, pret of French
prêt-à-porter, ready-to-wear, ready-to-go,
primed to depart — a feeling you've worn
for an entire lifetime. You see:
the difference between a flight and a life
raft is just the amount of baggage space
            and an arrival hall
without a face you know
is just another room
you learn to make a home out of.

Always too much time to kill
at the boarding gate, yet
not enough for living someplace
before running into
the next expiration date.
Every holiday season a eulogy
for moments missed. Here: fold your limbs
inward, like a human paper crane
into this middle seat. If you stay
            perfectly still   you can hear
the low hum of timezones
turning under the plane wing.

            After takeoff
you press the call button by your seat
and six thousand miles away
your mother stirs in the loosening dawn,
phone screen still aglow; fingers reaching —

It is nearly midnight on this
side of the world and I am le
arning how to fold 云吞 from a
pair of hands flecked with white, by
which I mean, yes, it is snowing in the
kitchen again. *The trick to keeping these
wrappers separate,* unstickied, *is to flour every
thing generously.* We start by flattening mounds
of dough into flat circles — thin edges, thicker cen
ters, each alabaster round   ready   to cradle a
delicate balance   of   meat and
green. I   seam each
                                         wrapper

edge
with faint
palm imprints,
featherlight tributaries
criss-crossing. *The trick to
keeping* 云吞 *intact during the boil
is to not overstuff these wrappers,* or
else delicate skin will splinter into transl
ucent streams of dough ribbons unspooling
chunks of minced pork & celery, wrapper flap
ping like an empty wound. Skin here a vessel
for fill   ing — stuffing to fullness, like
when I overeat, as if I
could gorge myself on
loneliness the same way
one might feed herself in
to belonging. Onscreen, fingers
sew neat pleats, *one/two/pinch,* and in
my kitchen I bring my hands together,
cupping the dough like an offering, god, all
I ever wanted was to be held
— *like this.*

we failed earth

You are sitting
        a Scrabble board
                across me
and are making your thinking-hard face.
I am trying to will you away
            from the opening by the   Triple
                                              Word
                                              Score

I don't know if it's working, but I know
that sitting here with you is enough
of a win already.
I'm not as competetive as you think I am
but I enjoy the way it spurs you.
The trick is in the overlaps.
Right now, I can set   POLLEN
over your   FLOWER
        because scrabblewordfinder.org

        tells me that P/E and O/R are valid words.

Your hand hovers over the   top right corner
of the board, my breath pinched
with the tile between your fingers. You set down an   L
on a blank space.
I am relieved because the corner is mine for the taking.   O
    You change a STRIP into STRIPE as you spell out   N
                                                    E
                                                    L
and bag 42 points. You shake your shoulders   Y
in celebration of being in the lead. I feign applause
and we are both laughing.
        This is the only thing that matters.

instagram reels

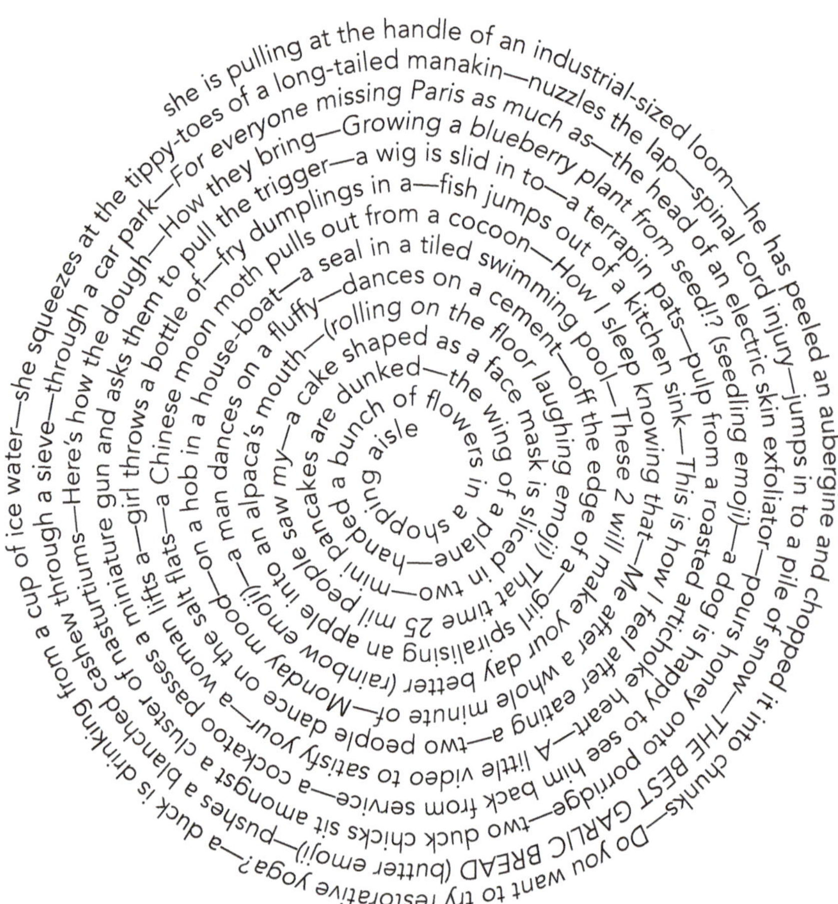

FICTION
31 AND OVER

> **ARTIST**
> Dora Maar, 1907 - 1997
> **TITLE**
> Untitled (Hand-Shell)
> **YEAR**
> 1934
> **MEDIUM**
> Gelatin silver print on paper (photo, photomontage)
> **DIMENSIONS**
> 401mm x 289 mm
> **COLLECTION**
> Centre Pompidou, Musée national d'art moderne, Paris

Henriette Théodora Markovitch is gone. I cut her out, excise her from the past. The artist Dora Maar now takes her place.

I cut around the edges, glue her in.

The camera – Rolleiflex – is now my eye. Advertisements and glossy fashion shoots. But give me time and I will give you more. My Rolleiflex looks out to see the world. My lens eye looks inside, trained on the mind. I'll leave the advertisements far behind. I'll give you things you only saw in dreams. I'll give you *Ubu roi* made flesh, made real.

I want the world to know my art, my self. I want these men to know my name. They gather in the Deux Magots, so pompous and self-sure and vain. Their heads turn to the pretty waitress though. They cannot help themselves.

> *"SURREALISM, n. Pure psychic automatism, by which it is intended to express, verbally, in writing, or by other means, the real process of thought.*
>
> *"Have professed absolute surrealism: Messieurs Aragon, Baron, Boiffard, Breton, Carrive, Crevel, Delteil, Desnos, Eluard, Gérard, Limbour, Malkine, Morise, Naville, Noll, Péret, Picon, Soupault, Vitrac."*

– André Breton

So it's a boys' club. Quelle surprise.

Me? I bring my wit and sharpen it. I gnash my teeth at them and growl.
They sip their coffee, simper, smoke their pipes. They turn their backs
and scratch each other's pelts, inscribing manifestos with male pride. I
clear my throat and speak again. Louder, with a deeper hue this time.
My gelatin-silver tongue tip wets my words. This time they listen, sit up
straight, and look. This time they claim they want to know my name.

II

ARTIST
Dora Maar 1907 - 1997
TITLE
29 rue d'Astorg
YEAR
1937
MEDIUM
Gelatin silver print on paper enhanced with colour
(photo, photomontage)
DIMENSIONS
294mm x 244mm
COLLECTION
Centre Pompidou, Musée national d'art moderne, Paris

I'm flying now my name is Dora Maar. They didn't think it could be done this way. I showed them how, and how I did it too. Their manifestos can be changed, it seems. My photomontage gives them something new. My visions hang on walls around the world.

I want the world to know my art. Is this the one I will be known for most? I name it for my studio's address. An anchor to the real, to Dora Maar. Unbeautiful, unconscious, uncanny. The statuette is mute. It can't be me. But it's the best I've ever done, I'm sure.

Then, once upon this time, I meet the man. The man is more than mortal. Demi-god. The Minotaur. Forbidden and desired. I long to find him deep in the labyrinth. I sharp my blade, my tool that cuts out dreams. Once more I cut around myself, my shape. But now it's all for him, a performance.

> *"the young woman […] kept driving a small pointed pen-knife between her fingers into the wood of the table. Sometimes she missed and a drop of blood appeared between the roses embroidered on her black gloves … Picasso would ask Dora to give him the gloves and would lock them up in the showcase he kept for his mementos."*

> **– Jean-Paul Crespelle**

He has my blood before he touches me. I give this sacrifice to him freely.

ARTIST
Pablo Picasso 1881–1973
TITLE
Femme en pleurs / Weeping woman
YEAR
1937
MEDIUM
Oil paint on canvas
DIMENSIONS
608mm × 500 mm
COLLECTION
Tate

He tells me that I give him back himself. He tells me I'm his muse, and so I am. Master, mistress, master, muse: the power. I lap it up. I lick it clean. I cut it round. I glue it down. My lens eye sees and makes and all is light.

But for a time he needs me more. I stop.

He calls me to his studio: I go. I sit for him. I lie for him. I laugh for him. I weep for him. His brushes turn my eye sockets to slits. My greenish pallor breaks, with white and blue for jagged fingers at my lips. The red hat looks obscene. I prostitute my pain to his desire. He paints on purple bruises to my skin.

I let his brushes make this woman weep.

> *"For years I've painted her in tortured forms, not through sadism, and not with pleasure, either... It was the deep reality, not the superficial one ... Dora, for me, was always a weeping woman ... And it's important, because women are suffering machines."*

> **– Pablo Picasso**

Thirty times his brushes make me weep. A Greek chorus of my disordered face. Together we bear witness to his art. No gallery could host us all at once. No white walls could hold our wails and sobs. The scrape and whine of rusted metal flesh. We suffering machines. The world is watching thirty mouths of mine. I want the world to know my art. But the sounds I make are music made by him. Genius is never silenced, or not his.

> *"Picasso is a man and a woman deeply entwined... He's a living ménage. Dora is a concubine with whom he is unfaithful to himself. From this ménage marvellous monsters are born."*

– Jean Cocteau

And now this *Femme en pleurs* is always me. It's my face disarranged and monochrome in Spain; the mother weeping after bombs have dropped. I hold the dead child, scream under Guernica's sky.

(This is his well-honed cruelty at play. His other lover bore the child for him - her womb's a fertile place to paint inside. Inside my womb is ash and smoke and rocks. That dead child never was.)

> *"I wasn't Picasso's mistress, he was just my master."*

– Dora Maar

Today he makes me put my camera down. The wreckage of *Guernica* is complete. My lens eye captures everything for him. His masterpiece is there in black and white. He says that they should be my final shots. The Minotaur has spoken, and that's that. My advantage must not stand. He can't stand it. I must replace my lens eye for his brush. I cut round it and let it drop. I am to paint, like him; he knows I'll fail. He knows I'll not compete in oil, I'll drown. I swim in seas of salts and silver waves. I do not fight him; I take up the brush. At least for now, the Minotaur is right. I paint.

IV

> **ARTIST**
> Dora Maar 1907 - 1997
> **TITLE**
> The Conversation
> **YEAR**
> 1937
> **MEDIUM**
> Oil paint on canvas
> **DIMENSIONS**
> 1620mm x 1300mm
> **COLLECTION**
> Private collection
> (Fundación Almine y Bernard Ruiz-Picasso para el Arte)

Two figures sit, a table, chairs, a light. This time I make sure I face away. You see my back, my neck, my head, my wrist. If I am weeping, you would never know. His other lover, her flat face is there. She's always there. That bitch will never leave.

I show him and he loves the work. He laughs. A sacrificial aphrodisiac. He's hard. We fuck. My camera falls. It cracks.

(Marie-Thérèse, I paint you plain. You're not. Allow me just that little joy, a salve. But I made space for you in what I make. We sit so close, too close, under the glow. Our bodies speak through him, his touch on us. But then you come one day and make him choose. You are a fool. We lived like this. It would have done.)

"I liked them both, for different reasons: Marie-Thérèse because she was sweet and gentle and did whatever I wanted her to, and Dora because she was intelligent ... I told them they'd have to fight it out themselves. So they began to wrestle. [It's] one of my choicest memories."

– Pablo Picasso

V

ARTIST
Dora Maar 1907 - 1997
TITLE
Paysage du Luberon
YEAR
1957
MEDIUM
Oil paint on canvas; signed on the reverse (left)
DIMENSIONS
460mm x 380mm
COLLECTION
Private collection

Nine years I cut around myself for him. And nine years more have passed since he has gone.

The Minotaur took off one night for good. Some other maze, some other sacrifice. The chorus in my head became too loud. I'm going to shock your brain now, Lacan said. The paddles singed my scalp, I wept real tears. The smell of burning hair was there for days.

The voices of the thirty mouths grew quiet, replacing faith in pain with faith in hope. Atoning for my sins, there is more peace. God knows I need it. God knows what I need.

These days I stay within the landscape of my mind. The world still watches thirty mouths of mine. The sounds I make are scores composed by him. Genius is never silenced, or not his.

I only want the world to know my art. And so I paint (until I die, I'll paint). I do not drown in oils, I thrive. I live, and will live like this still for years. I'll even swim in seas of salts again. No lens this time: only the negatives. It suits me to experiment anew.

I pray, and take my profit from his art. In nine years he gave me a decent haul. Sometimes, I pick a canvas, and I sell. The highest bidders value me as well. I keep the Chanel suit in the wardrobe. You come to ask me questions? It goes on.

"On the walls of a gallery, maybe they're worth only half a million. On the walls of Picasso's mistress, they're worth a premium, the premium of history."

– Dora Maar

Muse or mistress, master, slave, no matter. I am an artist. Not a weeping woman.

"All portraits of me are lies. They're Picassos. Not one is Dora Maar."

– Dora Maar

rearview mirror

So much happens beyond the edges of the mirror. Conversations without faces. Voices and silences. Sometimes eye contact in the glass. How's your night going? Busy shift? But most do not. Nights are best. Nights are worst. So many small worlds. Like a mussel seen through the crack where the shell splits before you break it open. This is a between time; always between places; other people's destinations, futures. There are things you can do and say when everything is paused. Rules belong to places, and

you are not there yet. Rules are for faces, and you cannot see mine. An eyebrow, an eye, half a nose, half my lips. And you, only an elbow, a knee, a handbag, a small dog perhaps. Tans, tattoos, football t-shirts, beards, flags, placards. LCOME OME or LACK IVES TTER. A bottle of wine, a bookcase. Rucksacks and wheelie cases. Children who won't sit down. Takeaway boxes in plastic bags with the handles tied. Or the smell of vinegar as chips spill onto the floor. Sometimes the mirror is filled with flowers and fingers. Or heels in hands, dangling by the straps, bare feet on seats. Outside the frame

are all the things I'll find afterwards: earrings, empty cans, food trodden into the floor, handbags, wallets, scarves, umbrellas, paper bags full of wrapped gifts, backpacks, beer bottles, unused tampons, sunglasses, single gloves, women's shoes, tights, empty condom wrappers, five-pound notes, coats, train tickets, boarding passes, lipstick, polaroid photos. A young woman asleep, hair covering her face, an empty champagne bottle held loosely in her hand. No bubbles left. Snoring. But it isn't afterwards often.

a complete algorithm in ada
for making an ada (lovelace)

```ada
with Ada.Text_IO; use Ada.Text_IO;

procedure Making_Ada is
type Years is range 1815 ... 1852;
subtype Daughter is Years range 1815 ... 1852;
subtype Wife is Years range 1835 ... 1852;
subtype Mother is Years range 1836 ... 1852;
type madness is (romanticism, incestuousness, excessiveness,
indecency);

perceived : Natural;
Byrons_madness : madness;

begin
 perceived := 0;
 for year in Years loop
   Byrons_madness := madness'Val(perceived);
   if year in Daughter then
     Put_Line ("Lady Byron was obsessed with the Lord's inheritable
" & madness'Image(Byrons_madness) & " so she made her daughter
study mathematics.");
     if year = 1827 then
       Put_Line("The golden <mean> is the desirable middle between
two extremes. Nothing to excess. Nothing to deficiency. It would be
madness to say the <mean> of a spiteful mother and a distant father
was anything other than a gross <mean> error, but they didn't have
pocket calculators yet.");
         Put_Line("In the classroom, Daedalus tells her: if God had
<mean>t women to fly, he would have given you wings. He maps a
path between sea and sky, tells her it's the only way. Ada does not
heed him. <mean> absolute difference. Her father melted to blood
in the sun and his best friend drowned. Ada wasn't afraid of water.
Unlike her father, she was an excellent navigator.");
         Put_Line("She investigates different materials for wings:
paper, oilsilk, wires, feathers. She examines the anatomy of birds
to determine the right proportions. Feathered ends justify the
<mean>s. She plans to surmount mountains, rivers, valleys, cut
across the country by a route most direct. A <mean> to an end.");
```

        elsif year = 1833 then
        Put_Line("In the classroom, Aristotle tells her courage is a virtue, but in excess would manifest as recklessness. In deficiency, cowardice. Well, she was just seventeen, you know what I <mean>? Who wooed in haste, and <mean>s to wed at leisure. Lady Byron hushed it up, but the tutor's particular style of calculations had left its mark. Love <mean>s never having to say you're sorry. Never being sorry <mean>s never <mean>ing to say you love.");
        Put_Line("Ada (a mathematician and a poet) remarks to Mary (a mathematician and a poet) that when many formulae undergo a transformation it is impossible to identify that the first is like the other because of their exceedingly dissimilar forms. Mary frowns, seeing the tutor's <mean> errors in Ada's calculus.");
        Put_Line("<mean>while, in the classroom, Coleridge (a poet) and Poincaré (a mathematician) talk over one another and the general hubbub of distinguished men. "Beauty," one says, and we are not sure which but it does not matter because the other will say much of the same, "is unity in variety! Science is nothing else than the search to discover unity in the wild variety of our experience." The other doesn't hear but, as has been remarked, says much of the same. Outside it is dark. Neither notice they're in a room of mirrors.");
        elsif year = 1840 then
        Put_Line("In the <mean>time, in the classroom, Socrates echoes Aristotle with example. Exclusive practice of gymnastics (recommended for the suppleness of ladies) will breed a <mean> spirit. An exclusive devotion to music (recommended for the accomplishment of young ladies) will produce a temper of effeminacy. And effeminacy is a <mean> business to be in.");
        Put_Line("SOCRATES: Any kind of mixture that does not possess a measure of the nature of <mean> will necessarily corrupt its ingredients and itself. For there would be no blending in such a case but really an unconnected medley, the ruin of whatever happens to be contained in it.");
        Put_Line("(Love letters sewn inside a bodice wilting with age and the bodice slowing dyed grey with sweat and ink until the equations within are unbalanced and the paper tears at the integral.)");

```
      Put_Line("ADA: And if effeminacy is the deficiency of man,
does that <mean> the <mean> of man is necessarily unwomanly and
a woman nothing but <mean>ly deficient?");
   elsif year = 1842 then
      Put_Line("(Charles, I think this machine could do more. What if
a number could represent entities other than quantity?)");
       Put_Line("SOCRATES: But now we notice that the force of the
good has taken up refuge in an alliance with the nature of the
beautiful. For measure and <mean> manifest themselves in all areas
of beauty and virtue.");
          Put_Line("(Charles, we could find objects whose mutual
fundamental relations could be expressed by those of the abstract
science of operations.)");
      Put_Line("ADA: What of coastlines? Coastlines are beautiful. But
I see no measure or <mean> in self-similarity. The limit is infinite.");
          Put_Line("(Supposing, for instance, that the fundamental
relations of pitched sounds in the science of harmony and of
musical composition were susceptible of such expression and
adaptations.)");
         Put_Line("SOCRATES: But we said that truth is also inclined
along with them in our mixture?");
       Put_Line("(The engine might compose elaborate and scientific
pieces of music of any degree of complexity or extent.)");
        Put_Line("ADA: We have said nothing. It is <mean>ly not the
<mean> of anything but self-affinity.");
      Put_Line("(Charles?)");
      Put_Line("SOCRATES: Well, then, if we cannot capture the good
in one form, we will have to take hold of it in a conjunction of
three: beauty, proportion and truth. Let us affirm that these should
be treated as a unity, for goodness is what makes the mixture good
in itself.");
      end if;
      if year = 1843 then
          Put_Line("(Note G: one, minus a half, a sixth, minus one
thirtieth.)");
       Put_Line("(Charles, I feel like we're getting nowhere.)");
       end if;
    end if;
```

```
   if year = 1851 and year in Wife then
      Put_Line(“In Ada’s new breakfast room, the headlines claim
that of course men get paid more, on average. By fair <mean>s or
foul. The <mean> includes footballer bonus payments. It’s the very
definition of <mean>. Ada does the calculations on the linen and
shakes her head. She bets on the game. Loses. Of slender <mean>s,
has to confess all to her husband. She tries to explain her model,
that this outcome was unlikely but possible.”);
   end if;
   if year = 1852 then
    if year in Mother then
      Put_Line(“She needs more time. She’s only thirty-six. Her
children are a <mean> of fourteen and two thirds. Her children are
a <mean> fourteen and two thirds. Although she is by no <mean>s a
better mother.”);
    end if;
    if year in Wife then
      Put_Line(“On her deathbed, she whispers to her husband the
secret she kept between whalebone and ribs for twenty-four
years. Her husband abandons her bedside, a <mean> three months
before her death.”);
    end if;
    if year in Daughter then
      Put_Line(“ther makes her atone, tells her the <mean> life
expectancy for a woman born in 1815. Ada knows it’s a <mean>
misuse of mathematics from a woman who will live her life twice.”);
      Put_Line(“It is no <mean> feat to <mean> what you say when
what you say is a <mean> absolute deviation of what you lived.”);
      Put_Line(“She asks to be buried next to the father she never
knew. Death <mean>s never <mean>ing to say you’re loved.”);
      Put_line(“She knew when she was twelve she could not grow
wings but it didn’t matter because she <mean>t to build them.”);
     end if;
    end if;
    perceived := (perceived + 1) mod 4;
  end loop;
end Making_Ada;
```

death considered as an exchange of post-it notes

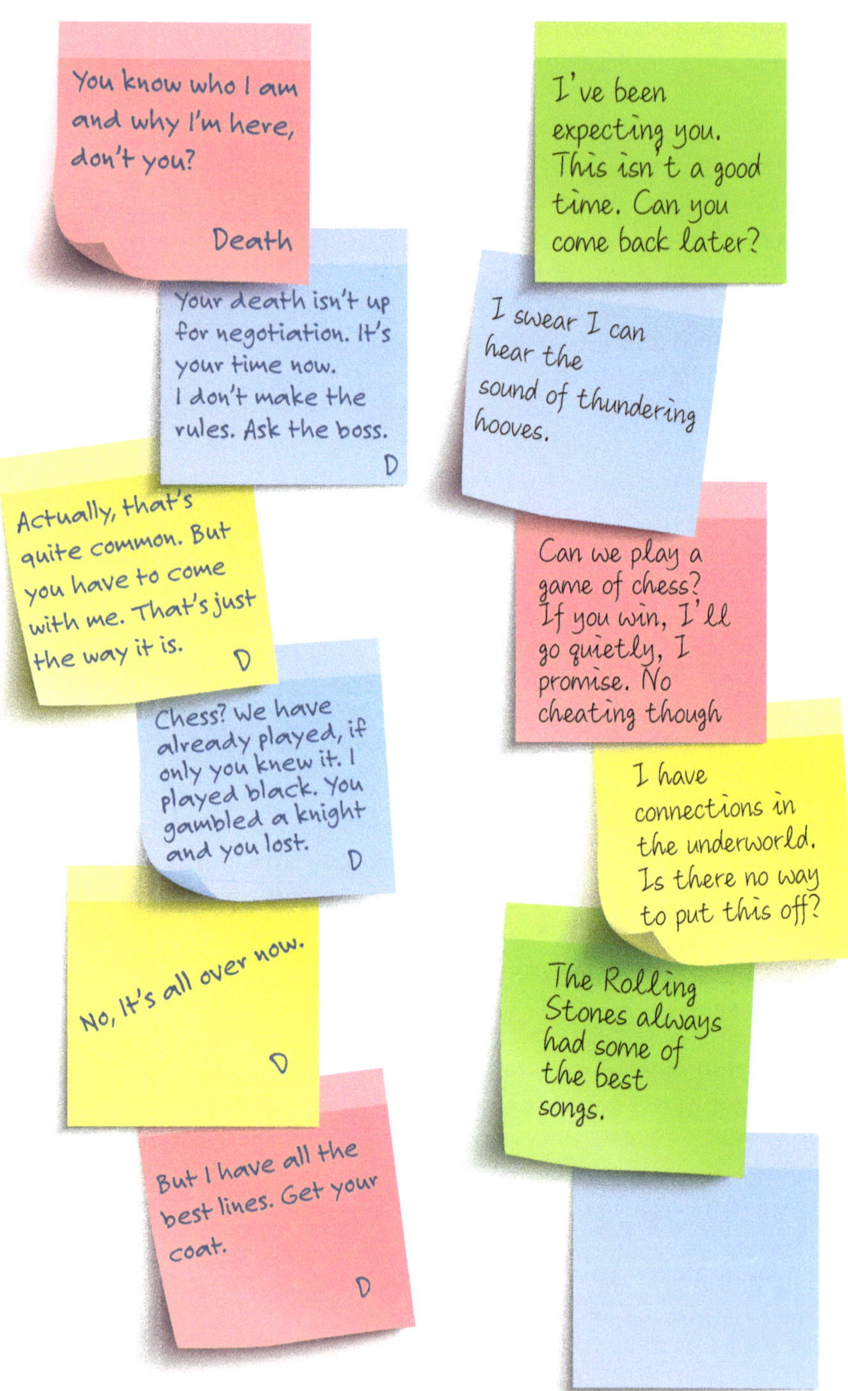

Hey, I feel like I missed your call.
So … ringing you back.
It's been too long. Hasn't it?
I've been reading that book, stolen from your shelf when leaving for London.

That awful one, about knights in castles swinging magic swords. It really is terrible. Like you said — confusing and weirdly written, but kinda fun. And it reminds me of you.

I'm at work right now. Out in the shed. With dumpsters and rats, and the rain. Furtively hiding. Furiously smoking. Rinsing my tongue and teeth in coffee to stay awake. I've been drinking to sleep. Then drinking to speak. Hiding from panic nestling behind my ears. Whispering and chittering, you won't make enough this year. You will be deported. From my love, my life and my home. To my not-anymore-home.

The flavour of smoke and swill stagnate on my lips. It tastes like — well it tastes like … ? Pretzels?

I buy them sometimes on my way home, homesick. They're different. Not the ones we bought on my tenth birthday. From the man, you knew from the factory. Shoving sacks, big as bodies, into the trunk of our car. Driving between jobs one and two that afternoon. Joking, we carried it into our apartment. We could curl up and hide inside, you said, I thought that would be a good idea then. I wish we had. And laughed over tears when crumbs sprayed between missing teeth to spell 'best birthday ever.'

Days with laughter were better than ones with eviction notices or termination letters. You could wrap one arm around me and say something stupid to cut through. Teaching me to do the same. Laughter became our secret sword. We used to fight them back from our door. The landlords, the bad bosses, and the bill collectors.

And that worked. Until it didn't.
Nobody tells you debt is a hereditary disease. A preexisting condition, disqualifying from employee healthcare plans.

The cancer spread so fast.

And you didn't laugh at choked on jokes when I carried you from our car into the hospital. My arms could hold you above the ground. Above those branches and the birdhouses we built, because you said don't they need a home too? Fingers dark with thickened blood, knotted and grew roots through the holes they tore in my t-shirt. Sweat staled in the clinical air of the waiting room. Apricots and plums, the trees we had planted to drop their fruits into baskets and jars of jam. When did we switch sizes? I choked out as we sat down inside.

Forced a laugh and hoped it would help. How could it?
You should have come sooner, they scolded.
But we couldn't afford it.

I smoked by the dumpsters and drank the coffee there too. Tasting neither.

The nurse had combed your wild nest into a neat sweep, while I helped you shave. And you almost looked like I had always remembered. Like pictures of you and mom at your wedding, before we met. At the end. At home. For two weeks I wanted you to die. I feel so guilty for that. Never one to drag something on. You could not eat. Pain leaked through the floorboards when the morphine ran out. I could not sleep. I would have to go back to work soon. Our sick days had all been used. There was no moon and city light strangled the stars. You whispered my name with crickets and I ran from my restless bed to yours. You said it again and looked up. So terribly lucid, so horribly calm.

I'm dead.
No, you aren't. You're Dad. I laughed again but I didn't mean to.
You snorted. Well? How do you know!?
Because you're still talking.
Arms folding in with new strength. Well, now I'm not! Then blew a raspberry and we laughed our bellies full again. You drew your sword and went back to sleep.

That was the last time we spoke, I guess.
Anyway, I'm almost finished with the book I swear. I haven't had much

time to read or grieve with work and everything. Speaking of, I have to go now. I can't hide too much longer. My break is probably over. Maybe I can bring it back to you, once I'm finished. We can eat the fruit as it falls from the orchard fed by your ashes. We can laugh about how bad it all was.

Alright, love you. Bye.
Thbbbt!

picture perfect

The wall looked boring, that's why I put the painting there. My husband disagreed.

"It clashes, it takes up too much space." He waved an arm. The anniversary bracelet jingled. "No one wants to walk in and see that."

"I do."

"I swear," he sighed, "if not for your obsession with paintings, you would be the perfect wife."

He said this a lot. Just swap 'your obsession with paintings' with 'your x'. There. Home-cooked guilt-trip from my husband. Hide it in a cupboard so tomorrow you can say *here's one I made earlier.*

The flat was nice. Big. Old tenement, only one other flat on the same floor, and that one was unoccupied. So no noise from the right, and the kids could run around as much as they wanted.

On the day Nichelle moved in next door, my husband helped her carry desk chairs and sock boxes and computer monitors. I heard them walking up the stairs, and I heard them going into her flat, but every time I tried to bob out and see them only my husband was there. Nichelle was always conveniently inside. She never said hi. A hermit, I guessed. Well, fine with me. Quieter.

I did see Nichelle in passing, eventually. Well. She passed. I stood stock-still.

"Manny," I hissed once back inside. My husband looked up. "Manny, what was that?"

"What is it, sweetie?"

"Our neighbour. I just saw our neighbour."

"Oh! She's pretty, isn't she?"

I didn't know whether to be flattered or offended.

"Pretty? That's all you have to say?"

"What else would I have to say?"

"Manny," I said. "She looks *exactly like me*."

"What? No, she doesn't."

"Yes, she does." The eyes, the nose, the hair. The same slight limp. Same birthmark on the wrist. "Do you think I don't know my own face when I see it?"

"Trick of the light," my husband suggested.

"She doesn't look like you. I would've told you."

Accepting that I was less interesting than the newspaper he'd shoved in his face, itbetterhavebeenbloodyinterestingbecauseI justannounedhavingadoppelgänger, I got back to looking into nannies for the kids. Every one had been a no so far, and at times of stress I liked to at least pretend to do something productive.

My mind kept straying to Nichelle. A twin? No, not a twin. As horrendous as this next sentence is going to be, I have seen a video of my own birth, because my parents were Like That. And let me tell you, there was definitely just one of me on that video. Everyone always said there's someone out there who looks like you. Fluke of genetics. But that wouldn't explain the limp, or the birthmark, or the overwhelming dread and terror I got from looking at her. And what would be the odds that a person like that would move in here, anyway? Doubles are meant to be halfway across the world, not

halfway across a corridor.

Maybe I really did imagine it.

Nichelle wasn't in when I knocked on the door,

nor did she answer the phone number that my

husband had stuck on the fridge. The next time I

saw Nichelle was when I came home earlier

than I said to meet the elusive nanny my

husband had hired because my tastes ran 'too

fussy'.

"Oh," I said. "Sorry, I think I got mixed up." My

stupid brain genuinely had me looking twice at

the corridor despite holding a key which had

successfully opened the door. "I thought this

was my flat."

"Aw, Mika, you're a riot!" It was the first time I

had heard Nichelle speak, and I did not like it.

She didn't sound like me. Much too chirpy for

that. Nasty undercurrent. "Come in, come in."

"I don't need to be told to come in to my own

home."

I couldn't stand her laugh.

"What are you doing here?" I asked, already knowing the answer. Nichelle smiled with her teeth. I've always smiled with my mouth firmly closed.

"Surprise! I'm your nanny."

"No you're not."

"Well, okay, your kids' nanny. If you want to be pedantic." She looked me up and down. "You seem the pedantic type."

"It can't be her," I said to my husband as soon as he stepped in the door. The rain stuck to his jacket dripped.

"Manny, it can't be her."

"Hello, Mika. Nice to see you, Mika."

"It can't be her," I said again. "She wouldn't leave when I asked her to, I had to pay her extra to fuck off next door. That's not normal, is it? A nanny's supposed to be bouncing at the chance to leave."

"What is your problem with Michelle?"

"I don't have any problems with Michelle, because I don't know who that is. *Nichelle*, on the other hand … "

CondescendinglittleamusedfacelikeI'msomestupidkido rananimalthatdoesn'tknowanybetter –

"Her name is Michelle, honey. M for Minnesota, Mississippi, Massachusetts –"

"I think I would've noticed if our next-door-neighbour was an American state," I snapped. My husband told me that I must've misheard when he first told me her name, because it was definitely, and always had been, Michelle with an M.

Michelle with an M kept being our nanny, and I kept hating it. Sometimes I'd come home to the kids in bed and Michelle cozied up to my husband, a glass of wine each. I didn't want to be *that* wife. I couldn't stand to be *that wife*. But come on. You see it, I saw it, it was plain as my own face. She wanted him. She wanted *this*.

A conversation, left on repeat:

"You have to sack her."

"No."

"Really, Manny. She creeps me out."

"You're overreacting."

"She's identical to me and you're

having wine in the evenings."

"She looks nothing like you, and

we're just friends. She gets bored

sitting in that flat all day. She gets

lonely. This is her only job, you know.

We can't do that to her, she'll have to

move out. Don't be so cruel."

"Without this job how could she even afford to move

in, huh?"

"Not really our business, is it, Mika?"

"A woman with my face is my business. I want to know

why she's here."

"We're not sacking her."

Rinse.

I came home one day to holes in my lovely paintings. Cables running through, so many cables. I couldn't believe it. I wanted to cry. Our plugs were stuffed, extension chords strewn. Leaching.

"I'm sorry, honey," my husband said. "But her electricity's out, so I said she could use ours. She needs her computer for work, you know."

"I thought we were her only job."

"Not now."

"So we can sack her."

"We're not sacking her."

"But my paintings," I said, almost a keen, a wail. "My paintings, Manny, why did you have to go through the paintings –"

"You said you didn't want her in here when the kids are at school. I was just respecting your wishes." He didn't even make eye contact with me. Couldn't be bothered. "Those paintings were ugly, anyway. If anything this is an improvement."

I invited Michelle over for dinner so that I could tell her to get her fucking cables out of my house. She never answered the door if I knocked, she only answered Manny, and never when I was there. I had to get her to come round.

My husband called her 'darling Micheline'.

"Michelle's short for Micheline," she said when I asked, draining the last of her glass. My husband has also finished. I was nowhere near. "Well, not really, but the full thing's such a

mouthful. I was thinking of

switching back, though. It's

much fancier, don't you two think?"

"Yes," my husband said. I put my head in my hands.

The cables remained, and every time I tripped on one I wanted to scream. More of her stuff was coming through the walls, all through holes, all because I wouldn't let up the rule of her coming round when it was just her and him, and I refused to let that up.

Her water turned off and she made a hole in her bathroom so she could reach through a grab our shower. I went to use the kettle and her hand was there, navigating it through to her side, and then it kept sitting there no matter how many times I pulled it back.

I hope it was her making all the holes. Rather her than him. Rather the mirror of her reaching through to my lamp plug as I did then – then –

The kids liked her more than

me. They liked her more than

me. They cried when she left

for the evening.

"Honeybear," my husband said

to me one night. His wine glass

was empty. The holes in the

walls were so big that a human

could fit through. "I have to tell

you something. It's about

Michaela."

"Micheline," I said. Quiet, defeated. "I thought her name was

Micheline."

"She's changing it. Suits her better, I think."

"Why does she look like me." Not even a question anymore.

"Manny, why does she look like me."

"She doesn't. But, uh, speaking of wives and their looks." He

hadn't introduced me to her when all three of us first spoke.

But he'd introduced her to me. That should've been a sign. A

mark of importance. I knew, I knew, but I didn't want to.

"The thing is, I want to be with Michaela." The tap was

dripping. It was on her side. "Romantically."

"I understood that you meant romantically."

"Good." He cleared

his throat. "Well, with

that out of the way –"

"You can't do this to

me. *She* can't do this

to me."

"She isn't doing

anything."

"She's stealing my

life."

He pitied me. "You're just upset. Maybe you should go to bed. One

last time in a king-sized one, eh?"

"Where are the kids? Manny, where are the kids?"

"Hmm? Oh, Mika's taken them to the cinema. She gets a work

discount. Nice of her, right?"

"I'm Mika. Manny, I'm Mika."

"Nickname for Michaela, hun."

"She can't have that too. She can't have my name too."

"I can't hear you, babe, you're speaking so quiet –"

No.   I'mnotbeingquietyouhorribleyoutraitoryouyouyouyouyouyou –

Yo.

Y.

I have the walls repaired.

The kettle, the shower, the plugs, all back where they belong. One house. One apartment. One family.

"Oh, darling Mika," Manny says. "I love it when you smile. Hold on, let me get a camera, I want that smile saved. All your lovely teeth."

"Perfect. We'll get them printed out. I know just where to put them."

I do.

I reach up.

I take down the paintings.

I started Saturday by scrolling Twitter, then Instagram. I didn't shower or dress. I had a poo. Having stared at my feet for some time on the toilet, I worried that the nail of my big toe was shrinking back into its cuticle. When I wiped my arse, my middle finger split through the toilet paper and I got poo on my finger. I skipped breakfast and watched an hour-long YouTube compilation of kids fighting. I started to dread Monday. I scrolled Pornhub for fifteen minutes. I masturbated to a subtitled video of a Japanese orgy. I was distracted by the captioned phrase, "Sucks dick like a black-toothed phantom." I scrolled Twitter, then Instagram. I checked my emails knowing there would be nothing of interest on a weekend. Only junk was new. For lunch, I had a big mug of instant coffee and half a pack of out-of-date Oreos. I intended to text my friend to say hello. I waited for the window cleaner to arrive. I hid from the window cleaner, crawling from room to room as they encircled my house. For tea I had 14p noodles with some frozen peas chucked in. I watched a film that I don't remember the name of. It was about guns and cars, and police were goodies. I scrolled Instagram, then Twitter. I dreaded Monday. I went to bed and dreamed of terrorists taking the office hostage. I fought them off, single-handedly, and saved everyone. I woke up in the middle of the night, needing a pee. I didn't go to the toilet for fear of the dark and images I concocted within it of a black-toothed phantom. I started Sunday by scrolling Twitter, then Instagram. I dreaded Monday. I didn't shower or dress. I had a poo. My toenail looked neither better nor worse. Something to keep an eye on. I had cornflakes for breakfast. I wrote a song in my head about walking around town wearing my flip flops. I repeated it over and over, so I wouldn't forget it. I watched a few episodes of a kids' T.V. show called Butt Ugly Martians hoping it would rekindle the joy and excitement it inspired in me as a child. It was much more simplistic and less artistic than I remembered. I decided to draw my own cartoon character. I ended up drawing a fox with a big human dick. I masturbated to a video of someone doing a pee while they looked into their webcam. I kicked myself for forgetting my song about flip flops. For lunch, I had a big mug of instant coffee and the other half of the pack of out-of-date Oreos. I scrolled Instagram, then Twitter. I watched a lot of Eastern European stop motion animations about death and the indignities of living. For tea I had oven chips with a mint cornetto for pudding. I watched a film about cars and guns, and the police were baddies. I forgot what it was called. I scrolled Twitter, then Instagram. I dreaded Monday. I went to bed.

would you like to add a gift message?

Would You Like to Add a Gift Message? ☑

Russell Hobbs 19750 Rice Cooker and Steamer, 1.8 Litre, Silver

Shipping to: The Meyers, 7 Mainsfield Road, Roethumpton, Bergh, JS8 2XT

Estimated Delivery *3-5 working days*: 4th August, 2018

Gift Receipt ☑

Gift Message:

> Hey newlyweds! Are you recovered from the wedding?! It was a wonderful time and you two are the perfect couple! (Jealous!) And congratulations on the new home – I don't think I'll ever be able to afford the deposit haha. Well, enjoy the cooker! My mum recommended it so if it's terrible you can blame her. She misses you already but she's closer to Joe's famous curry anyway. I'd get you the 20000 Cooker instead but you didn't make me a bridesmaid – JK. Keep in touch – lots of love
>
> -Louise xxx

AA Driving Theory Test & Highway Code (AA Driving Test) (AA Driving Test Series) Paperback

Shipping to: Louise Braderfield, Martleshin Flats 225, 1A, Westring, BS37 7SU

Estimated Delivery *Next Day Priority Delivery*: 16th August, 2018

Gift Receipt ☐

Price: £9.15

Include message to recipient? Yes ☐ No ☑

Sprinkle Flame Candle Happy Birthday Tin, Pink

Shipping to: Marie Braderfield, 18 The Pirors, Roethumpton, Bergh, JS8 2QH

Estimated Delivery *Next Day Priority Delivery*: 2nd September, 2018

Gift Receipt ☑

Gift Message:

> Happy Birthday mum! (Hopefully not belated). Sorry I couldn't be there - who knew Bergh would get so popular? At least you've got everyone keep you company – they'll treat you. Especially Max. Couldn't make your fave red velvet cake so I hope you like this candle instead. It's meant to smell like cake (not red velvet, but maybe there's a market for that?!) – I know you normally burn incense but I couldn't get that next day. Anyway, I'll give you a call soon. Don't be a stranger!
>
> - Lou

----

2 Items -

Expert Dog Training: "Think Like a Dog" Here's Exactly How to Train Your Rescue: 1st Edition 2018

5 Feet Elastic Dog Lead Strong Rope with Highly Reflective Threads

Shipping to: Louise Braderfield, Martleshin Flats 225, 1A, Westring, BS37 7SU

Estimated Delivery *1-2 Days*: 4th September, 2018

Gift Receipt ☐

Message to Driver:

Hi, got a new dog and it seems to hate noises... and delivery men. Please DON'T ring the doorbell! There's a space in the garden by the bins where you can leave the package, just the road is tight. I promise Henry is friendly, but I just don't want another complaint from the neighbours!

- Louise

A Perfect Rose Moment Gift Set | 1x 187ml Rosé and Glass, 3 x double fudge chocolates, 1 x pair cosy socks

Shipping to: Louise Braderfield, Martleshin Flats 225, 1A, Westring, BS37 7SU

Estimated Delivery *Next Day Priority Delivery*: 5th September, 2018

Gift Receipt ☑

Gift Message:

Hey me – you'll get through this. L <3

Louise Braderfield
Martleshin Flats 225, 1A
Westring
BS37 7SU

Invoice: 1698002 | 17/09/2018

Narla's Women Spaghetti Strap Criss Cross Tie Back Dress - Black, Size 16 with gift message:

hey girl, good luck on the date tonight! (FINALLY) here's the dress I know you'd never buy for yourself – i think the black will look slimming on you, but I went a size up as I know you eat when you're stressed. just imagine me there hyping you up as always! of course, if you actually get out of westring you might have more luck finding 'the one'… also sorry to hear about harry. anyway, onwards and upwards! don't complain about the dress being 2 sexy, you need to put yourself out there. anyway, you can return it using the online form if it doesn't fit, but I know it will! p.s, joe has been taking cooking classes and we read loads about how dangerous rice cookers can be – so that's out the window – thanks anyway babes xxx

Enjoy your gift! From: jessie meyers

Durex Extended Pleasure Condoms, 2 x Pack of 12 Condom

Shipping to: Louise Braderfield, Martleshin Flats 225, 1A, Westring, BS37 7SU

Estimated Delivery *Next Day Priority Delivery*: 22nd September, 2018

Gift Receipt ☐

Price: £14.22

Include message to recipient? Yes ☐ No ✓

BARLAST Floor Free Standing Lamp

Shipping to: Max Erudine, 12 Jackson Walk , Westring, BS37 7EW

Estimated Delivery *1-2 Working days*: 23rd September

Gift Receipt ☐

Price: £46.77

Include message to recipient? Yes ✓ No ☐

> Hey! Thanks for having me round last night. Anyway, I'm totally sorry about being such a clutz – I didn't realise high heels could fly that far or that I shouldn't try that flamingo move. I hope this is the right kind of lamp – it was pretty dark so I couldn't tell what your original one looked like. Fingers crossed you recover quickly too, my brother is nearly a qualified paramedic so can give you some tips about healing 'down there' quickly. How romantic… I've totally ruined this. Well – I have your address but realised you have nothing about me so here's my number if you did want to stay in touch. 07786202679. If you didn't, I'd totally understand.
>
> - Louise x

Choose Items to Return

- **Russell Hobbs 19750 Rice Cooker and Steamer**
- ○ **Sprinkle Flame Candle Happy Birthday Tin**
- ○ **5 Feet Elastic Dog Lead**
- ○ **Expert Dog Training: "Think Like a Dog"**
- ○ **A Perfect Rose Moment Gift Set**
- ○ **Durex Extended Pleasure Condoms, 2 x Pack of 12 Condom**

Reasons for return:

> Product is no longer needed
>
> Neither are the condoms but oh well
>
> *ERROR: Character limit exceeded (-36/26)*

Fuaensm Spider Catcher | Extra Long Handle With Bristles for Indoor and Outdoor use, 65cm

Shipping to: Louise Braderfield, Martleshin Flats 225, 1A, Westring, BS37 7SU

Estimated Delivery *Next Day Priority Delivery*. 1st October

Gift Receipt ☐

Price: £12.59

Include message to recipient? Yes ☐   No ☑

Act-Tive Yoga Exercise Floor Matt in Blue, Large Padded Extra Thick 12mm Non-Slip With Carry Straps

Shipping to: Hetty Wilmur, 13 Ardune Close, Westring, BS37 7GH

Estimated Delivery *Next Day Priority Delivery*: 7th October

Gift Receipt ☑

Gift Message:

> Hey Hetty, Thanks for the lift to class – it really cleared my head and it was so great to meet someone. I didn't know my bum could fold like that! I'd really like to take you up on that dinner offer? So sick of making myself jacket potatoes or noodles each evening. I mean, I really would like to see you again outside of the gym (priorities). It's just so great to speak to someone…Now I sound desperate! Back on topic, I noticed your matt needed replacing. I don't think you should be breathing in little blue bits when doing downward dog – I've gone with this company before and they're great. Hope this isn't too forward. I think I remember hearing that blue was your favourite colour? Have fun with it and I'll see you for our next session/date!
>
> - Louise x

3M Littmann Classic III Monitoring Stethoscope, Gray Tube, 69 cm, 5621

Shipping to: Jason Braderfield, 13b University Avenue, Roethumpton, Bergh, JS8 8PH

Estimated Delivery *Next Day Priority Delivery*: 26th October, 2018

Gift Receipt ☑

Gift Message:

> YOU DID IT! I'm so proud of you bro – now the most qualified in the family! :) thanks for getting a degree so that the attention is on you. Didn't want to get you a cringy balloon arrangement - These were the ones you needed for placement right? West Bergh Ambulance Service are going to be so lucky to have you. I would be too, if I wasn't so far away. Did I tell you – I'm so clumsy that I injured a boy I was seeing? Anyway, I'll be sure to ask you about every weird lump and mole. I can already hear you moaning about how that's not what you do – I know you just lift old ladies out of bed ;). Rather you than me. Enjoy these – they better be right, they cost a fortune! Please do message. I literally have no clue what's going on with anyone down there. Enjoy the ceremony and photoshop me in!
>
> Love Lou

Letterbox Flowers and Herbal Tea Set | Colour: Tiffany Blue

Shipping to: Joseph Braintree, Reshwild Care, Sutherwold, Bergh, JB9 2XS

Estimated Delivery *3-5 working days*: 9th November

Gift Receipt ☑

Gift Message:

> Grandad you numpty! Jason told me about his call out – I was just saying how lucky it was that you had him around. Well I bought you this to help you with recovery. If only you lot lived closer to a train station! Thinking of you at this time too, I know it's getting close to that date. Hopefully these flowers won't make you sneeze like the last time. Please keep me updated on the scans, I'm always the last to know. And join in with the movement classes – they'll help!
>
> -Lou xx

Condol-essences Co – Guardian Angel Necklace (Silver/326) with Luxury Gift Bag & Card

Shipping to: Marie Braderfield, 18 The Pirors, Roethumpton, Bergh, JS8 2QH

Estimated Delivery *1-2 Working Days: 12th November*

Gift Receipt ☑

Gift Message:

> Hi mum, just wanted to send something to say I'm so proud of you and I know Grandma would be too. Miss you loads right now. Let me know how the lanterns go tonight – I'll light a candle for her. And maybe have a glass of wine too… Please check in on Grandad if you can. Just don't sing that song with the horses in it! She hated that one haha. Please call me soon!
>
> - Lou

Eliminating Intrusive Thoughts: Reasons to Stay by Denny Howull | Polar-bear- Publishing

Shipping to: Louise Braderfield, Martleshin Flats 225, 1A, Westring, BS37 7SU

Estimated Delivery *Next Day Priority Delivery*: 13th November

Gift Receipt ☑

Gift Message:

> Hey me – Let's keep trying. L <3

Choose Items to Return ⌐
                                                    ↳

           ○   **Sprinkle Flame Candle Happy Birthday Tin**
           •   **5 Feet Elastic Dog Lead**
           •   **Expert Dog Training: "Think Like a Dog"**
           ○   **A Perfect Rose Moment Gift Set**
           ○   **Durex Extended Pleasure Condoms, 2 x Pack of 12 Condom**
           ○   **Fuaensm Spider Catcher**
           •   **Act-Tive Yoga Exercise Floor Mat**
           ○   **3M Littmann Classic III Monitoring Stethoscope**
           ○   **Letterbox Flowers and Herbal Tea Set**
           ○   **Condol-essences Co – Guardian Angel Necklace**
           ○   **Eliminating Intrusive Thoughts: Reasons to Stay by Denny Howull**

Reasons for return:

> Product/s no longer needed
>
> Might invest in a cat. Fuck this.
>
> ERROR: Character limit exceeded (-32/26)

Jelly Belly 15360 3D Jewel Collection Air Freshener - Very Cherry

Shipping to: Louise Braderfield, Martleshin Flats 225, 1A, Westring, BS37 7SU

Estimated Delivery *3-5 Working Days*: 19th November

Gift Receipt ☐

Price: £2.49

Include message to recipient? Yes ☐ No ☑

----

3 Items

A4 Padded Bubble Envelopes Bags Postal Wrap Envelopes

GBoss 1 Inch Thank You for Supporting My Small Business Stickers, Roll of 500pcs,Labels & Mailing Supplies for Small Business

2 Pack Business Card Holders, 2 Tiers Acrylic Card Display Desk Stand Holder

Shipping to: Louise Braderfield, Martleshin Flats 225, 1A, Westring, BS37 7SU

Estimated Delivery *3-5 Working Days*: 29th November

Gift Receipt ☐

Price: £27.98

Include message to recipient? Yes ☐ No ☑

---

2 Items

Packin- Tape Brown 6 Rolls 48mm x 50m General

JerryPackaging 10 Large Double Wall Cardboard Moving House Boxes 45.7cm x 30.5cm x 30.5cm with Carry Handles and Room List

Shipping to: Louise Braderfield, Martleshin Flats 225, 1A, Westring, BS37 7SU

Estimated Delivery *Next Day Priority Delivery*: 11th December

Gift Receipt ☐

Price: £28.99

Include message to recipient? Yes ☐ No ☑

Athena Artificial Christmas Tree Xmas Pine Tree with Solid Metal Legs Perfect for Indoor and Outdoor Holiday Decoration (Green, 7FT)

Shipping to: Louise Braderfield, Sutherwold, Bergh, JB9 2XU

Estimated Delivery *Next Day Priority Delivery*: 19th December

Gift Receipt ☐

Price: £19.99

Include message to recipient? Yes ☐ No ☑

Louise Braderfield
Sutherwold
Bergh
JB9 2XU

Invoice: 129003 | 01/01/2019

Cat Collar with Bell and Bow Tie, Quick Release Safety Buckle Collars for Kitten and Cats, Soft Tartan Design (Black & White) with gift message:

> Sending this next day as Jessie and Joe told us you'll be out partying! So glad you made friends in Bergh so quickly. We love having you here. We wanted to get you something for your business but you're all set – we're so proud of you! Anyway, here's a little holiday present for Clover instead – who knew you'd be such a cat person?! We love you so much Lou – see you when you're back xxx
>
>
> Love Mum, Jason and Grandad

shortlisted writers

Rosa Chalfen
Viktoria Dakill
Abdullah Asad Iqbal
Megan Holland
Petra Palkovacsova
Sapphire Jones
Dominique Gracia
JP Seabright
Kathanne Easton
Max Henninger
Richard Moon
Catherine O'Neill
David Wright
Teo Eve
Jack Cooper
Yvette Naden
Elspeth Wilson
Haley Jenkins
Siobhan Dunlop
Gabrielle Cracknell
Aysegul Yildirim
Imogen Davies

Maritsa Baksh
Arden Fitzroy
Sarah James
Joyce Walker
Lynda Nash
Michał Kamil Piotrowski
Charlotte Ljung
Rachael Charlotte
L Kiew
David Felix
Nathan Evans
Kirsty Fox
S K Grout
Claire HM
Steven Antalics
Al Crow
Ilias Tsagas
Rosaleen Lynch
Katie Margaret Hall
JE Rowney
Kayleigh Cassidy

Story
Machine
Productions

www.ingramcontent.com/pod-product-compliance
Lightning Source LLC
Chambersburg PA
CBHW050045040726
47599CB00015B/1798